KETO SMOOTHIES

FOR BREAKFAST AND SNACKS

Delicious & Energy Boosting Smoothies

For Weight loss

KetoSky

deemed liable for any hardship or damages that may befall them after undertaking information described herein. Additionally, the information in the following pages is intended only for informational purposes and should thus be thought of as universal. As befitting its nature, it is presented without assurance regarding its prolonged validity or interim quality. Trademarks that are mentioned are done without written consent and can in no way be considered an endorsement from the trademark holder.

Table of Contents

MANGO SMOOTHIE I

Ingredients

- 1/2 cup peeled, pitted and sliced fresh mango honey to taste 1/2 cup ice
- 1/2 cup orange juice

How To

- ✓ Place the juice, fruit and honey in a blender.
- ✓ Blend on high speed for 30 seconds.
- ✓ Add the ice and blend until smooth.

MANGO GINGER SMOOTHIE

Ingredients

- 2 ripe mangoes, peeled and chopped
- 2 pieces crystallized ginger, about 1 ounce
- cup nonfat buttermilk
- One 8-ounce container nonfat vanilla yogurt
- Handful of chipped ice

How To

- ✓ In a blender, purée the fruit and ginger, scraping down the sides as necessary. Add the buttermilk, yogurt and ice and purée until smooth and frothy.
- ✓ Serves 2

MANGO MANIA SMOOTHIE

Ingredients

- cups nonfat vanilla yogurt 1 cup mango nectar
- 2 mangos, peeled and chopped
- 1/4 tsp. cardomom

How To

- ✓ Add all ingredients to blender and process until smooth. Add 1 cup of ice cubes and blend till crushed and smooth.
- ✓ Serves 2

MANGO PEACH SMOOTHIE

Ingredients

- 1 large peach (about 8 oz.), peeled, pitted, and cut into chunks
- 1 cup peeled mango chunks
- cup peach nectar
- tablespoons lime juice

How To

- ✓ Combine all ingredients in blender and blend until smooth.
- ✓ Makes two small drinks.

MANGO TANGO SMOOTHIE

Ingredients

- 1 cup pineapple juice
- 1 cup orange juice
- 1/2 frozen banana (chunks)
- 1 cup pineapple sherbet

How To

- ✓ 1 1/2 cups frozen mango slices Pour all liquid ingredients into the blender.
- ✓ Add all frozen ingredients.
- ✓ Blend at MIX setting for 30 seconds then blend at SMOOTH setting until smooth.
- ✓ While the machine is running, move the stir stick around counter-clockwise to aid mixing.
- ✓ Serve immediately.
- ✓ Each recipe serves 3-5.

MEGA SMOOTHIE

Ingredients

- mango -- peeled, seeded and chopped
- bananas -- peeled and chopped
- 8 large strawberries
- 2 medium carrots -- chopped
- 2 cups ice cubes
- 1 tablespoon honey
- 1 cup yogurt -- optional

How To

- ✓ In a blender combine half of each ingredient, including: mango, bananas, strawberries, carrots, ice cubes, honey and yogurt and blend until smooth.
- ✓ Pour into a glass and serve immediately.
- ✓ Repeat process for remaining ingredients.
- ✓ Yield: 2 servings

MELON MADNESS SMOOTHIE

Ingredients

- 1 1/2 cups seeded and chopped watermelon
- 1 1/2 cups seeded and chopped honeydew melon
- Juice of 2 limes
- cup vanilla nonfat yogurt
- 1 cup ice cubes

How To

- ✓ Place all ingredients in a blender and blend until smooth. Pour into glasses.
- ✓ Makes 4 servings

MELON SMOOTHIE

Ingredients

- 1 1/2 cups seeded and chopped watermelon
- 1 1/2 cups seeded and chopped honeydew melon
- Juice of 2 limes
- 1 cup vanilla lowfat yogurt
- 1 cup ice cubes

How To

- ✓ Place all ingredients in a blender and blend until smooth.
- ✓ Pour into glasses.
- ✓ Yield: 4 servings

MUCHO MELON SMOOTHIE

Ingredients

- 1 cup of peach fat-free yogurt, frozen
- 1 cup skim milk
- 1/2 cup cantaloupe
- 1/2 cup honey dew melon
- 4 ice cubes
- 1/2 cup strawberries (or substitute with watermelon)

How To

✓ Put yogurt, milk, and strawberries into blender.

✓ Blend on high for about 30-45 seconds.

✓ Then add in cantaloupe, melon, and ice.

✓ Blend once again on high for 1 minute.

NECTARINE SMOOTHIE

Ingredients

- 1/4 cup orange juice
- 1/2 cup plain, low-fat yogurt
- 1/2 cup peeled, pitted and sliced nectarines honey to taste

How To

- ✓ Place all the ingredients in a blender.
- ✓ Blend on high speed until smooth.

NECTARINE BERRY SMOOTHIE

Ingredients

- 1 nectarine, pitted
- 3/4 cup strawberries, hulled
- 3/4 cup blueberries, rinsed and drained
- 1/3 cup nonfat dry milk powder
- 1 cup crushed ice

How To

- ✓ In a blender combine nectarine, strawberries, blueberries, milk powder and crushed ice.
- ✓ Blend until smooth. pour into glasses and serve.
- ✓ serves 2

LOW-FAT LOW CALORIE STRAWBERRY BANANA SMOOTHIE

Ingredients

- 1 Banana
- Maui Wowi
- Recipe for a refreshing day-If you can't get a Maui Wowi, here is the next best thing.
- 1 Cup Fresh Strawberries
- 1 cup Non-fat yogurt
- packet sugar or sugar substitute
- cups ice

How To

✓ Blend until creamy

ORANGE BANANA CREAM SMOOTHIE

Ingredients

- 1/4 cup orange juice
- 1/4 cup pineapple juice
- 1 tbsp coconut milk
- 1/2 banana
- 1/4 tsp grated fresh ginger root
- 1/2 cup crushed ice or 2 small ice cubes

How To

✓ Add all ingredients to blender and process until smooth.

✓ Serves 1.

ORANGE FRUITY SMOOTHIE

Ingredients

- 1 medium banana, peeled and cut into
- 1-inch pieces
- 1 ripe peach, peeled, halved, pitted, and diced
- 1 cup raspberries
- 1 1/2 cups freshly squeezed orange juice
- 3 ice cubes

How To

✓ Combine all ingredients in blender and whip until smooth.

✓ Serves 2

ORANGE PINEAPPLE COCONUT SMOOTHIE

Ingredients

- 1 tbsp coconut milk
- 1/4 cup pineapple juice
- 1/4 cup orange juice
- 1/2 banana
- 1/4 tsp grated fresh ginger root
- 1/2 cup crushed ice or
- 2 small ice cubes

How To

✓ Add all ingredients to blender and process until smooth. Serves 1.

ORANGE SMOOTHIE I

Ingredients

- 2 oranges, peeled & sectioned
- frozen banana, chunked
- ¼ c. orange juice
- T. yogurt

How To

✓ 1 tsp. vanilla Blend in blender until smooth.
✓ Serves 2.

ORANGE FRUITY SMOOTHIE

Ingredients

- 1 ripe peach, peeled, halved, pitted, and diced
- 1 medium banana, peeled and cut into
- 1-inch pieces
- 1 cup raspberries
- 1 1/2 cups freshly squeezed orange juice
- 3 ice cubes

How To

- ✓ Combine all ingredients in blender and whip until smooth.
- ✓ Serves 2

PAPAYA SMOOTHIE

Ingredients

- 3/4 cup peeled, seeded and chopped ripe papaya honey to taste
- 1/2 cup ice
- 1/2 cup orange juice

How To

- ✓ Place the juice, fruit and honey in a blender.
- ✓ Blend on high speed for 30 seconds.
- ✓ Add the ice and blend until smooth.

PAPAYA BERRY SMOOTHIE

Ingredients

- 1 frozen banana (freezing it makes the drink super cold without diluting it with ice)
- 10-12 raspberries (fresh or frozen)
- 1/2 c water or fruit juice
- 1/2 fresh papaya
- 1 tbsp toasted wheat germ (optional)

How To

✓ Puree in blender 30-45 seconds. makes about sixteen delicious, filling, vegan, nutritious ounces.

PAPAYA NECTARINE SMOOTHIE

Ingredients

- 1 cup Crystal Light or any other sugar-free lemonade
- 6 oz. fat free peach yogurt, frozen
- (This is one container of Yoplait)
- 1 nectarine, pitted and unpeeled
- 1 cup papaya, seeded and peeled

How To

- ✓ Put all ingredients into blender.
- ✓ Blend well until smoothie consistency is reached!

PAPAYA RASPBERRY SMOOTHIE

Ingredients

- 1 frozen banana, peeled
- 1/2 fresh papaya
- 10-12 raspberries (fresh or frozen)
- 1/2 cup water or fruit juice

How To

- ✓ Put all ingredients into blender.
- ✓ Blend until smoothie consistency is reached!

PEACH BERRY SMOOTHIE

Ingredients

- 1 cup nonfat peach yogurt
- 3/4 cup peach nectar
- 1/2 cup raspberries
- 1/2 cup ripe medium peaches, diced

How To

✓ Combine the yogurt and nectar in a blender. Add the raspberries and peaches.

✓ Blend until smooth. Serves 2

PEACH CINNAMON SMOOTHIE

Ingredients

- tablespoons firmly packed brown sugar
- ripe peaches
- cups nonfat plain yogurt
- 1/4 teaspoon ground cinnamon
- 1 cup ice cubes

How To

✓ In a 2- to 3-quart pan over high heat, bring about 1 quart water to a boil. Immerse peaches in boiling water for 15 seconds; drain. When peaches are cool enough to touch, in 1 to 2 minutes, peel, pit, and cut into chunks. In a blender, combine peaches, yogurt, brown sugar, and cinnamon; whirl on high speed until smooth, about 1 minute.

✓ Add ice and whirl until smooth, about 2 minutes longer.

✓ Pour into tall glasses (at least 16-oz. size). Serves 2

PEACH MELBA SMOOTHIE

Ingredients

- 1/4 cup fresh or frozen raspberries
- 1 cup peeled, sliced peaches
- 1 cup chilled peach juice
- 1/2 vanilla yogurt
- 3 ice cubes

How To

✓ Pour all items in a blender and blend until smooth.
✓ Pour into 2 glasses and garnish with fruit. Serves 2.

PEACH REFRESHER

Ingredients

- 1 cup vanilla frozen yogurt
- 2 cups peach nectar or apple juice
- 1/2 banana
- 1 cup peach yogurt

How To

- ✓ 1 1/2 cups frozen peach slices
- ✓ Pour all liquid ingredients into the blender.
- ✓ Add all frozen ingredients. Blend at MIX setting for 30 seconds then blend at SMOOTH setting until smooth.
- ✓ While the machine is running, move the stir stick around counter-clockwise to aid mixing. Serve immediately.
- ✓ Each recipe serves 3-5.

PEACHY APPLE SMOOTHIE

Ingredients

- 1 fresh peach
- 1/3 cup non-fat milk
- 1/4 cup of frozen apple juice concentrate

How To

- ✓ Peal 1 fresh peach.
- ✓ Cut it into thin slices.
- ✓ Put into a plastic bag with a zipper bag, laying flat. Put the plastic bag into the freezer for 1-2 hours.
- ✓ Take out 1/4 of the peaches and break them into pieces. Mix in a blender with 1/3 cup of milk and 1/4 cup of frozen apple juice concentrate.
- ✓ Cover and blend until smooth. pour into a glass, and add more peach slices for peachy ice cubes!

PEACHY BLUE SMOOTHIE

Ingredients

- 1 peach, frozen
- 1 cup light (reduced sugar) fat-free vanilla yogurt, frozen
- 10 blueberries, frozen
- 1/2 cup 1% milk
- 1/2 T. crushed pecan
- 1/2 tsp salt
- 1/4 tsp vanilla extract

How To

- ✓ Put all ingredients into blender.
- ✓ Blend until smoothie consistency is reached!

PEACHY COOLER SMOOTHIE

Ingredients

- 1 c Chilled peach nectar
- 1 Container (6 ounces) peach yogurt
- ½ c Milk
- Ground nutmeg

How To

- ✓ Place nectar, milk and yogurt in blender.
- ✓ Cover and blend on high speed about 30 seconds or until smooth. Sprinkle with nutmeg.
- ✓ 2 servings (about 1-1/4 cups each); 180 calories per serving.

PEACHY PUNCH SMOOTHIE

Ingredients

- 10 oz of apple cider
- 3-5 slices of peach
- 4 large strawberries
- 1 banana
- 1/8 tsp of cinnamon

How To

✓ Put all ingredients into blender.
✓ Blend well until smoothie consistency is reached!

PEANUT BUTTER BANANA SMOOTHIE

Ingredients

- Tbsp. reduced fat creamy peanut butter
- banana, frozen, cut in chunks
- cup skim milk
- 1/2 cup frozen vanilla yogurt or
- fat free ice cream

How To

✓ Mix in blender till smooth. Serves 2.

PEANUT BUTTER POWER SMOOTHIE

- 1/2 cup silken tofu
- 1/2 cup soy milk
- 1/3 cup creamy peanut butter
- bananas -- frozen
- 2 tablespoons chocolate syrup

How To

✓ Combine soy milk, tofu, and peanut butter in blender.
✓ Add bananas, chocolate syrup, and any ice cubes if desired.
✓ Blend until smooth.
✓ Serves 2.

PEANUT BUTTER SUNDAE SMOOTHIE

Ingredients

- Tablespoons honey
- 1/4 cup smooth peanut butter
- 1/3 cup milk
- cups vanilla ice milk
- 1/4 teaspoon wheat germ

How To

- ✓ Stir peanut butter, honey and milk together.
- ✓ Cook over low heat, stirring constantly.
- ✓ Remove from heat when peanut butter has melted; stir in ice milk and wheat germ; serve chilled.
- ✓ Serves 4.

PINA COLADA SLUSH SMOOTHIE

Ingredients

- 1-1/2 cups pineapple juice, chilled
- cups cubed fresh pineapple
- 1/4 cup cream of coconut (such as Coco Lopez)
- 1 cup ice cubes
- 1 cup vanilla fat-free frozen yogurt

How To

✓ Place pineapple into freezer; freeze until firm (about 1 hour).

✓ Remove from freezer; let stand 10 minutes.

✓ Combine juice and cream in a blender. With blender on, add pineapple and ice cubes, 1 at a time; process until smooth.

✓ Add yogurt; process until smooth.

✓ Serve immediately.

PINEAPPLE COCONUT SMOOTHIE

Ingredients

- 1 cup pineapple chunks, canned in juice, drained
- 1/2 cup buttermilk
- tsp. coconut flakes
- 1/2 tsp. coconut extract

How To

✓ Add all ingredients to blender and process until smooth.

✓ Serves 1.

PINEAPPLE DELIGHT SMOOTHIE

Ingredients

- 2 bananas, frozen and chunked
- 6 slices canned pineapple
- cups nonfat milk
- 1 tablespoon honey

How To

- ✓ In a blender combine milk, frozen bananas, pineapple and honey.
- ✓ Blend until smooth.
- ✓ Makes 4 cups, or 2 large servings.

PINEAPPLE BERRY SMOOTHIE

Ingredients

- pineapple rings (Dole pineapple slices)
- 6 fresh strawberries
- cup orange juice
- 1/4 cup pineapple juice
- 15 frozen raspberries
- 8-10 frozen boysenberries
- 12-15 frozen blueberries
- 3 oz. non-fat yogurt, any flavor (about half a container of Yoplait)
- Ice (however much you prefer for consistency)

How To

✓ Put all ingredients into blender.
✓ Blend well until smoothie consistency is reached!

PINEAPPLE ORANGE BANANA SMOOTHIE

- 6 oz. light (reduced sugar) fat-free peach yogurt, frozen
- 1 banana
- (This is one container of Yoplait)
- 6 oz. (1 can) Dole Pine-Orange-Banana juice

How To

- ✓ Put all ingredients into blender.
- ✓ Blend until smoothie consistency is reached! If drink is too thick, add orange juice.

PINEAPPLE PAPAYA SMOOTHIE

Ingredients

- 1/4 cup peeled, cored and cubed pineapple
- 1/4 cup peeled, seeded and chopped ripe papaya
  honey to taste
- 1/2 cup orange juice
- 1/2 cup ice

How To

- ✓ Place the juice, fruit and honey in a blender.
- ✓ Blend on high speed for 30 seconds.
- ✓ Add the ice and blend until smooth.

POWER FRUIT SMOOTHIE

Ingredients

- 1/2 cup hulled strawberries (don't need to cut them up)
- 1 frozen banana (best if cut into 1-inch -- chunks then frozen)
- 1/4 cup soy milk, orange juice or water cinnamon to taste

How To

- ✓ Add all of the ingredients in a blender.
- ✓ I start with 1/4 cup of liquid and add more depending on how thick I want the smoothie.
- ✓ Blend in spurts until smooth.
- ✓ Variations: * Use peaches, blueberries, apple slices, or more bananas in place of strawberries (or combine them!) May need to vary the liquid depending on the juciness of the fruit. * Use fresh bananas and 1-2 ice cubes * In addition to the cinnamon

✓ Add one or more of: nutmeg, cloves, ginger, vanilla

kwvegan vegan

✓ Serves 1.

POWER SMOOTHIE

Ingredients

- In a blender, combine 1/2 banana, 1/2 cup yogurt (I like vanilla flavored), 1/2 cup fruit juice (i.e. orange, cranberry, etc.).
- For added nutrition I use 1 Tbls. soy protein powder, 1 Tbls. molasses,
- 1 tsp. wheat germ. Blend until smooth.
- Then add frozen fruits, strawberries, raspberries, etc., one at a time, until smoothie is consistency you desire.

How To

- ✓ The basic recipe is: ice, fruit, yoghurt, juice and/or milk. (I usually stick to juice, but sometimes add just a splash of milk to smooth it out.)

PUMPKIN SMOOTHIE

Ingredients

- 12 ounces evaporated skim milk – chilled
- 1 3/4 cups pumpkin, canned -- chilled
- 1/2 cups orange juice
- 1/2 cup banana -- sliced
- 1/3 cup brown sugar, packed

How To

- ✓ Place all ingredients in blender and blend well.
- ✓ If desired, serve over ice and sprinkle with cinnamon.
- ✓ Serves 6.

RAINFOREST FUSION SMOOTHIE

Ingredients

- 1/2 banana
- cup frozen pineapple pieces
- 1/2 cup orange juice
- Tbsp. coconut milk
- 1/2 tsp. lime juice
- 1/2 cup nonfat frozen vanilla yogurt
- 1/2 cup ice

How To

- ✓ Combine ingredients in blender; mix until smooth and frothy.
- ✓ Serves 1.

RASPBERRY CAPPUCCINO SMOOTHIE

Ingredients

- 1/3 cup fresh-brewed espresso
- 3/4 cup chocolate milk, low-fat
- tablespoon chocolate syrup
- 1 1/2 cup nonfat coffee flavor frozen yogurt
- 1 cup raspberries
- 1/2 cup skim milk
- 1/4 teaspoon cocoa powder

How To

- ✓ Combine the chocolate milk, espresso, and chocolate syrup in a blender. Add the frozen yogurt and raspberries. Blend until smooth.
- ✓ Pour into glasses. Rinse out the blender container. Pour the milk into the blender and blend on high speed until frothy, about 15 seconds.
- ✓ Divide between the smoothies and sprinkle them with chocolate powder. Serves 2.

RASPBERRY CREAM SMOOTHIE

Ingredients

- 1 cup vanilla frozen yogurt
- 1 cup orange juice
- 1 cup raspberry yogurt
- 1/2 frozen banana (chunks)
- 1 1/2 cup frozen raspberries Pour all liquid ingredients into the blender.

How To

✓ Add all frozen ingredients. Blend at MIX setting for 30 seconds then blend at SMOOTH setting until smooth.

✓ While the machine is running, move the stir stick around counter-clockwise to aid mixing. Serve immediately. Each recipe serves 3-5.

RASPBERRY SMOOTHIE (LOW FAT)

Ingredients

- 1 pkt Weight Watchers Vanilla Smoothie
- 1 cup cold skim milk
- 1/2 cup fresh or frozen raspberries
- 5 ice cubes

How To

✓ Crush ice cubes in blender. Add smoothie mix and milk and blend. Add raspberries and frappe. If needed, add a packet or two of sugar substitute. Serves 1.

RASPBERRY SMOOTHIE I

Ingredients

- 1/4 cup orange juice
- 1/2 cup plain, low-fat yogurt
- 1/2 cup washed, stemmed raspberries honey to taste

How To

✓ Place all the ingredients in a blender. Blend on high speed until smooth.

RASPBERRY SUNRISE SMOOTHIE

Ingredients

- 1/2 cups orange juice
- 1 1/2 cups frozen raspberries
- cup raspberry sherbet
- Pour all liquid ingredients into the blender.

How To

- ✓ Add all frozen ingredients.
- ✓ Blend at MIX setting for 30 seconds then blend at SMOOTH setting until smooth.
- ✓ While the machine is running, move the stir stick around counter-clockwise to aid mixing. Serve immediately.
- ✓ Each recipe serves 3-5.

SAINT SMOOTHIE

Ingredients

- 3 nectarines, peeled and de-stoned

- 2 bananas, sliced

- cup nonfat vanilla yogurt crushed ice 2 Tbsp
  grenadine

How To

✓ Place the nectarines and bananas into a blender along
  with the yogurt and whisk it all together until it has a
  good consistency.

✓ Next, fill the glasses a quarter with crushed ice, and
  pour over the grenadine.

✓ Top the glass up the rest of the way with the smoothie
  mixture, and enjoy. Serves 2

SOUTHWEST SMOOTHIE

Ingredients

- 1/2 c Banana; sliced
- 1/2 c Mango OR papaya OR guava (Fruit should be of one kind listed and be chopped)
- c Milk
- 1 tb Honey

How To

✓ Place all ingredients in food processor workbowl fitted with steel blade or in blender container; cover and process on high speed until smooth. Strain if using mango. Serves 3.

SPARKLING FRUIT SMOOTHIE

Ingredients

- c Yogurt, plain or -fruit-flavored
- c Chopped fresh fruit
- Freshly grated nutmeg - pinch
- 2/3 c Ice-cold champagne, -sparkling water or ginger -ale
- Mint sprigs (opt) -OR Fruit slices (opt) -(for garnish)

How To

✓ Combine the yogurt, fruit, and nutmeg in a blender; process until smooth. Pour into glasses, filling 3/4 full.

✓ Top off with champagne, sparkling water or ginger ale. Gently stir to combine.

✓ Garnish with mint sprigs or fruit slices, if desired. Serves 2.

STRAWBERRY SMOOTHIE

Ingredients

- large strawberries
- oz. light (reduced sugar) fat-free strawberry frozen yogurt (This is one container of Yoplait)
- 4 oz. Crystal Light or other sugar-free lemonade
- 1 packet Equal sweetener or 2 teaspoons of sugar (1 gram)

How To

✓ Put all ingredients into blender. Blend until smoothie consistency is reached! Serves 1.

STRAWBERRY BANANA SMOOTHIE

Ingredients

- 1 cup frozen strawberries
- 1 cup frozen banana cubes
- cup pineapple juice -- or more if needed
- tablespoons cream of coconut
- 1 dash grenadine garnish: ripe strawberries

How To

✓ Combine all ingredients in a blender until smooth.

✓ Add more pineapple juice if needed.

✓ Serve immediately. Yield: 2 servings

STRAWBERRY BANANA SUPREME SMOOTHIE

Ingredients

- 1 cup strawberry nectar or apple juice
- 1 cup milk
- 1 frozen banana
- 1 1/2 cups frozen strawberries
- 1 cup strawberry yogurt
- Pour all liquid ingredients into the blender.

How To

- ✓ Add all frozen ingredients. Blend at MIX setting for 30 seconds then blend at SMOOTH setting until smooth.
- ✓ While the machine is running, move the stir stick around counter-clockwise to aid mixing. Serve immediately. Each recipe serves 3-5.

STRAWBERRY-BANANA TOFU SMOOTHIE

Ingredients

- ½ cup apple juice
- ½ cup frozen vanilla nonfat yogurt, peach sorbet, or desired flavor sorbet
- 4 ounces (1/2 cup) soft tofu, drained
- 1 cup fresh or frozen sliced strawberries or peaches
- 1 banana, broken into chunks
- 1 teaspoon honey
- ½ cup ice cubes
- Fresh whole berries for garnish (optional)

How To

✓ 1. Place the apple juice, sorbet, tofu, strawberries or peaches, banana and honey in a blender. Cover and process until well blended.

✓ 2. With blender still running, drop ice cubes, one at a time, through the hole in the lid until smooth.

✓ 3. Pour into tall glasses; garnish with a fresh berries, if desired. Makes 2 -3 servings

STRAWBERRY LEMON ZING SMOOTHIE

Ingredients

- cups lemonade
- 1 cup strawberry yogurt Pour all liquid ingredients into the blender
- 2 cups frozen strawberries

How To

- ✓ Add all frozen ingredients. Blend at MIX setting for 30 seconds then blend at SMOOTH setting until smooth.
- ✓ While the machine is running, move the stir stick around counter-clockwise to aid mixing. Serve immediately.
- ✓ Each recipe serves 3-5.

STRAWBERRY PEACH & PEAR SMOOTHIE

Ingredients

- 1 peach, stoned and sliced
- 1 pear, peeled, cored and chopped
- 200g (7oz) strawberries, frozen and slightly thawed
  good squeeze of lime

How To

✓ Put everything into a food blender and whiz until smooth. Serves 2.

STRAWBERRY PINEAPPLE SMOOTHIE

Ingredients

- 3/4 bag frozen unsweetened whole strawberries
- 1 cup orange juice (fresh-squeezed or Tropicana Pure Premium recommended)
- 4 cups Dole pineapple juice
- 1 1/2 cups lowfat vanilla yogurt, frozen

How To

✓ Put all ingredients into blender. Blend well, stopping to stir when necessary, until smoothie consistency is reached!

STRAWBERRY SOY SMOOTHIE

Ingredients

- 1 cup vanilla soy milk
- 5 ounces silken tofu, firm, chilled and cubed
- 2 cups frozen or fresh strawberries
- 2 tablespoons honey
- 1/2 teaspoon vanilla

How To

✓ Combine in blender. Makes 2 shakes.

STRAWBERRY ZEST SMOOTHIE

Ingredients

- 10 oz Frozen sliced strawberries -- thawed
- 4 c Milk
- 1 pt Strawberry ice cream
- 1 tsp Lemon rind -- grated

How To

✓ Combine all, one half at a time in blender on high, 1 min. (Or use a mixer). Serve in tall glasses. Serves 8.

SUNSHINE SMOOTHIE

Ingredients

- 1 cup orange sherbet (or substitute frozen yogurt)
- 1 1/3 cups pineapple chunks, fresh or canned in juice and drained
- 1 cup fresh strawberries, trimmed
- 1 1/2 cups sparkling mineral water

How To

✓ Blend first 3 ingredients in a food processor until smooth; add mineral water until blended. Serves 4

SWEET STRAWBERRY SMOOTHIE

Ingredients

- 1 strawberry/mango yogurt (any kind will do)
- 1 cup fresh strawberries, cut up (or you can use any kind of fruit that's in the yogurt you desire) ½ cup of sugar
- 1 cup chopped ice cubes

How To

- ✓ Combine the strawberries (or any kind of fruit) and sugar in the blender and mix on second speed into a liquid.
- ✓ Add the yogurt and blend until mixed thoroughly. Add the ice a little at a time until it's completely mixed. Enjoy!

TANGERINE BERRY SMOOTHIE

Ingredients

- ½ cup lowfat or nonfat plain yogurt
- ½ cup tangerine juice
- ½ cup frozen, unsweetened strawberries, unthawed
- 1 tablespoon sugar, or to taste

How To

- ✓ In a blender whirl all ingredients together 30 seconds to 1 minute until smooth and frothy. Makes 1 serving; about 1 - ½ cups.

TANGY SUMMER BLEND SMOOTHIE

Ingredients

- 1 nectarine
- 6 oz. light (reduced sugar) fat-free peach frozen yogurt (This is one container of Yoplait)
- 1/2 c. Dole Pine-Orange-Guava juice
- 1/2 c. Crystal Light or other sugar-free lemonade
- 1 packet Equal sweetener or 2 teaspoons of sugar -- (1 gram)

How To

✓ Put all ingredients into blender. Blend until smoothie consistency is reached! Serves 1.

TRIPLE FRUIT SMOOTHIE

Ingredients

- 1 banana
- 4 slices fresh or frozen peaches
- 4 fresh or frozen strawberries
- 10 ounces apple juice or cider
- 1/8 teaspoon cinnamon

How To

✓ Place all ingredients in blender. Blend until SMOOTH! Pour into chilled glass and garnish with fruit and a dash of cinnamon. Serves 2.

TROPICAL FIVE FRUIT BLAST SMOOTHIE

Ingredients

- large banana, peeled and cut into
- 1-inch pieces
- kiwi fruit, peeled and quartered
- 1/2 cup peeled and diced mango
- 1/2 cup peeled and diced papaya
- 1 cup freshly squeezed orange juice
- ice cubes

How To

Combine all ingredients in blender and whip until smooth. Serves 2

TROPICAL PARADISE SMOOTHIE

Ingredients

- 1 1/2 cups pineapple-orange juice
- 1 cup sliced banana (about 1 medium)
- 1 cup ice cubes
- 3/4 cup diced pineapple
- 1/2 cup vanilla fat-free frozen yogurt
- 1 tablespoon flaked sweetened coconut

How To

✓ Combine all ingredients in a blender, and process until smooth. Serve immediately.

TROPICAL PASSION SMOOTHIE

Ingredients

- papaya 1 peach
- passionfruit
- 150ml (5fl oz) freshly squeezed orange juice

How To

- ✓ Method Peel the papaya and remove the seeds, put the flesh into a blender. Wash the peach, halve, remove the stone and chop the flesh, then add.
- ✓ Halve the passionfruit and scoop the seeds straight into the blender with the orange juice.
- ✓ Blend. Serve poured over ice with the remaining passionfruit on top. Serves 2

TROPICAL SMOOTHIE

Ingredients

- 2 1/2 cups pineapple juice -- unsweetened
- 1 cup strawberries -- sliced
- 1 banana -- sliced OR mango -- diced OR papaya -- diced * If using mangos or papaya, make sure they are ripe.
- Peel and dice the fruit. Have the pineapple juice well-chilled.

How To

✓ Combine all ingredients in a blender. Puree until thick and very smooth. Serves 4.

TROPICAL TOFU BERRY SMOOTHIE

Ingredients

- I cup light (reduced sugar) fat-free vanilla yogurt
- 1 cup skim milk
- 1 banana
- 3" cube of soft tofu
- 3/4 cup blueberries
- 1 cup strawberries

How To

- ✓ Put yogurt, milk, banana, tofu, and Equal into blender and blend until smooth.
- ✓ Add berries and blend again until smoothie consistency is reached.

TUTTI FRUITY SMOOTHIE

Ingredients

- 1 cup sliced ripe banana (about 1 medium)
- 1 cup orange juice
- 3/4 cup sliced peeled peaches
- 3/4 cup sliced strawberries
- 1 tablespoon honey

How To

✓ Combine all ingredients in a blender; process until smooth. Serve immediately.

TWICE BERRY BANANA SMOOTHIE

Ingredients

- 1/2 ~ 1 cup yogurt
- 1/2 ~ 1 banana
- 1/2 ~ 1 cup blueberries (fresh or frozen)
- 1/2 ~ 1 cup strawberries (fresh or frozen)

How To

✓ Juice from one orange (when in a bind I have used orange juice from a carton) honey or sugar to taste. Mix in blender till smooth.

WAKE & SHAKE SMOOTHIE

Ingredients

- 3/4 cup orange juice
- 3/4 cup nonfat yogurt
- 1/2 of a medium papaya (peeled, seeds removed)
- 1 teaspoon lime juice
- 1/2 banana
- 3-4 ice cubes

How To

✓ Place all ingredients in a blender. Blend until smooth!
Serves 1.

YOGURT SMOOTHIE

Ingredients

- 1 Banana
- 1 1/2 cup Dannon Vanilla Yogurt (fat free)
- 3/4 cup frozen peaches
- 1 whole frozen strawberry container
- tablespoon orange juice concentrate

How To

✓ Place all ingredients in blender, add ice to fill blender and blend. Serves 2.

YOGURT FRUIT SMOOTHIE

Ingredients

In Blender Add:

- C Vanilla Yogurt (or fruit flavor)(I like Old Home brand)
- 1 Banana - cut up*
- 4-5 Strawberries*
- ½ tsp Vanilla or Almond Extract
- 1 Tbsp Sugar or Equal
- Enough Ice Cubes to fill blender loosely

How To

✓ Sometimes I freeze fresh strawberries and cut back on the ice. You can add more or less of any of the ingredients. *You can use whatever type of fresh fruit you like, approximately 1-1/2 - 2 C worth.

YOGURT SHAKE SMOOTHIE

Ingredients

- 1 Small Banana
- 1 T Frozen orange juice
- Sugar or honey, to taste
- 4 Ice cubes
- Yields about 2 1/2 cups.

How To

✓ Place all ingredients into blender or food processor. Whirl until smooth.

✓ Variations: Instead of banana, use l cup cubed melon, l/2 cup fresh or frozen berries, l/2 cup pineapple, l peeled and chopped kiwifruit or l/2 peeled and cored apple.

BAHAMA MAMA SMOOTHIE

Ingredients

- 1/4 cup plain non fat yogurt
- 1/2 banana
- 1/4 cup tofu
- 1 1/2 cups tropical V-8 Splash or other pineapple/citrus blend
- Frozen strawberries, pineapple, and mango water or soy milk to taste/consistency
  Optional:
- 3 or 4 baby carrots (you'll never know they're in there!) 1 tbs. wheat germ or 4-5 almonds

How To

✓ Blend all ingredients in blender until smooth.

BANANA-APRICOT SHAKE

Ingredients

- 1/2 cup low-fat milk
- 1 cup mashed ripe bananas -- (about 2 large), -- frozen
- cup apricot nectar
- 1/4 teaspoon vanilla

How To

- ✓ Place all ingredients in blender.
- ✓ Cover and blend about 30 seconds or until smooth.
- ✓ Serve immediately over ice cubes. Serves 2.

BANANA BERRY SMOOTHIE

Ingredients

- bananas
- 1/2 cup blueberries
- 1 cup plain yogurt

How To

- ✓ Peel bananas, slice and place on a cookie sheet.
- ✓ Put in freezer and freeze until solid.
- ✓ Remove from freezer and place in blender.
- ✓ Slice berries and add to blender.
- ✓ Pour in yogurt.
- ✓ Blend until smooth.
- ✓ Pour into glass and serve.

FROZEN BANANA SMOOTHIE

Ingredients

- frozen bananas
- Vanilla extract
- Sliced seasonal fruit

How To

- ✓ Cut frozen banana into 4 pieces and cut away peel and discard.
- ✓ In blender, blend banana until thick and smooth.
- ✓ Add a dash of vanilla extract and blend again.
- ✓ Scoop out and serve with fresh sliced seasonal fruit.

BANANA CINNAMON SMOOTHIE

Ingredients

- In a blender combine:
- 1/4 c skim milk
- 1/2 banana A splash of vanilla
- 1/4 c plain yogurt (I actually use vanilla for mine but it would depend on what else you're adding)
- A dash of cinnamon 4 ice cubes

How To

- ✓ Blend to desired consistency.
- ✓ Substitute whatever fruit is in season or even use something like canned peaches.
- ✓ I usually double the recipe above but this is what I remember the original measurements to be.

BANANA COFFEE SMOOTHIE

Ingredients

- 1/4 tsp. ground cinnamon
- 1 8-oz. container low-fat coffee yogurt
- 2 small bananas, peeled, cut up, and frozen
- 1 1/2 cups skim milk
- Dash ground nutmeg

How To

- ✓ In a blender container combine frozen bananas, milk, yogurt, cinnamon, and nutmeg.
- ✓ Cover and blend till smooth.
- ✓ To serve, pour into glasses.
- ✓ If desired, garnish with fresh bananas and mint.

BANANA CREAMA SMOOTHIE

Ingredients

- 2 teaspoons pure vanilla essence
- banana
- cups milk
- ½ cup natural yogurt

How To

- ✓ Slice banana and put into a blender.
- ✓ Add ½ cup milk, yogurt and vanilla.
- ✓ Blend until banana is mushed.
- ✓ Add remaining milk and blend until smooth.
- ✓ Pour into glasses.

BANANA LIME SUBLIME SMOOTHIE

Ingredients

- 1 cup lime sherbet
- 2 cups limeade
- 1 banana
- 1 cup ice Pour all liquid ingredients into the blender.
- 3 Tbs. coconut milk

How To

✓ Add all frozen ingredients.

✓ Blend at MIX setting for 30 seconds then blend at SMOOTH setting until smooth.

✓ While the machine is running, move the stir stick around counter-clockwise to aid mixing.

✓ Serve immediately. Each recipe serves 3-5.

BANANA MOLASSES SMOOTHIE

Ingredients

- 5 pitted prunes
- 1 medium banana, peeled and cut into
- 1-inch pieces
- 1/4 teaspoon ground cardamom
- 3 ice cubes
- 2 cups low-fat vanilla soymilk.
- 1 tablespoon blackstrap molasses

How To

- ✓ Place prunes in small bowl and cover with hot tap water. Let rest for 15 minutes or until plump.
- ✓ Drain. Combine plumped prunes and remaining ingredients in blender and whip until smooth.

BANANA ORANGE SMOOTHIE

Ingredients

- 1 8-ounce container nonfat cherry yogurt
- 1 banana, peeled, cut into pieces
- 1 orange, peeled, white pith removed, cut into segments
- 8 frozen dark cherries
- 6 frozen strawberries

How To

- ✓ Combine ingredients in blender.
- ✓ Blend on medium speed until smooth.
- ✓ Divide between 2 glasses.

BANANA PEACH SMOOTHIE

Ingredients

- 1 cup mashed ripe bananas -- (about 2 large), -- frozen
- 1 cup peach nectar
- 1/2 cup low-fat milk

How To

✓ Place all ingredients in blender.

✓ Cover and blend about 30 seconds or until smooth.

✓ Serve immediately over ice cubes. Serves 2.

BANANA PINEAPPLE COLADA SMOOTHIE

Ingredients

- 1/2 cup pineapple juice
- 1/2 cup ice cubes
- 1/2 peeled banana
- 1/2 cup pineapple chunks
- 1 tablespoon sugar
- 1/4 teaspoon coconut extract

How To

✓ Place all ingredients in a blender and blender until smooth.

BANANA SOY SMOOTHIE

Ingredients

- 4 bananas, frozen
- 1 tablespoon honey
- 3/4 cup soy milk
- 1/2 cup soft silken tofu
- 1 tablespoon vanilla extract
- 1 tablespoon carob powder

How To

- ✓ Combine soy milk and tofu in blender.
- ✓ Add bananas, honey, vanilla extract, and carob powder.
- ✓ Blend until smooth.

BANANA SPICE SMOOTHIE

Ingredients

- 1-2 teaspoons honey (to taste)
- 180ml cold milk (low fat or soy may be used)
- ripe banana, chopped
- tablespoons low fat natural yogurt

How To

- ✓ Place all ingredients, except nutmeg, into a blender and blend until smooth.
- ✓ Pour into a tall glass, sprinkle with nutmeg if desired and serve immediately.
- ✓ For a delicious nutty taste, try adding 1 tablespoon of slivered almonds to the blender.

CPSIA information can be obtained
at www.ICGtesting.com
Printed in the USA
BVHW090727230621
610212BV00009B/1154